STOP! PLAYING
THE DICE

Devices to Design Amazing Products

Anshuman Sharma

Dedication

To my beautiful daughters Gunn and Kli

To my lovely wife Nilam

CONTENTS

Introduction

The success of a company depends mainly upon the quality of the products it develops and sells in the market. A successful product needs to be unique and should be according to the requirements of the customers. A good product becomes its own marketer as every time it is used, it delights its users, which makes them the advocates of the product. We can observe this phenomenon in some of the winning products in the market. A winning product has great design, quality and gives satisfactory experiences to its users.

Few companies have mastered the art of product design and they are extremely successful in the market with high profitability and growth. These companies use the product design skills as their competitive advantage and protect it like trade secret. In fact, the process of creating great products is not complex. It is a set of tools and methods which, if used properly and sincerely, can support any design team to develop amazing products. We have tried to expose these methods and devices in this work.

To contrast the available books on product design methods, we have kept this book extremely simple. The specified devices can be used by any sincere person looking to design products. The simplicity of the devices is evident from the fact that even a layperson, with no knowledge about product design, can understand and use these devices. A successful product needs to be holistic, equipped with innovative marketing, superior quality and emphatic support. An innovative design of a product with weak support cannot get success in the market.

The products are differentiated by their value proposition, quality and features. An excellent product has great design, which evolves from the culture of the company where everybody is serious about design and focuses on improving it consistently. A great design evolves mainly from the attitude rather than technical expertise.

It has always been difficult for companies to create great products. Some companies hire highly qualified technical experts to create the magic, while others outsource the product design process. Sometimes the responsibilities of creating new ideas and products lie on few elite individuals, in other cases R&D department bears the complete responsibility of developing successful products. In most cases these efforts fail. The main reason for this failure is the wrong approach.

The most important aspect for developing new ideas about products and subsequently designing it requires a proper methodology, which is generally simple but effective. Every successful company has their set of method to design the products but the fundamental ideas remain same. This book tries to reveal the effective but simple methodology of designing the great products.

The methodology discussed in the book has four segments and is called READ Technique. READ stands for Research, Experience, Analyze and Discover. 'Research segment' focuses on capturing and analyzing the information available in the market, 'Experience segment' focuses on checking out the views and ideas generated, 'Analyze Segment' focuses on observing the aspects for product and 'Discover Segment' focuses on surveys and interviews. Each of the four segments has several devices and methods specified in this work which would help the professionals in designing a great and winning product.

To design a great product the designers need to focus on a specific area of the design process. The specified segments and devices in the book would serve the designers by focusing their attention to each area of the design process. Each device described in the book briefly describes it, specifies its importance & value, explain the way to use it and supported by an example to describe it.

The design devices list specified in this book is exhaustive and every device would not be suitable for your projects. Design team needs to identify and list the devices to be used for a specific project. These devices would motivate the design team in various ways by suggesting them relevant methods to solve the design problem.

It is suggested that this resource should be used as a guide and reference to create better product designs.

RESEARCH SEGMENT

Research segment of the READ Model includes the devices which focus on collecting and researching the available data, information, insights in archives, published or tacit format. This segment equips the designers with substantial grasp of the project to graduate to other segments of the model.

Device 1: Research - Scenario Analysis

Check with various scenarios to identify different ways which would create operational difficulties for the product.

This device would help the designer to identify the various situations when the product would be affected negatively with user's actions.

Identify various scenarios which can fail the product due to human actions. Find the reason for these failures. These can be through human mistakes, negligence or actions. The purpose is to design the product robust enough to protect itself for possible problems.

<u>Example</u>: Identify various ways when a glass container can break during its usage.

Device 2: Research - Salability

Check for the salability of the designed product.

This analysis is important as the designed product should be marketable and commercially viable.

Conduct a market survey asking the target segment about their intention to buy the product based upon product features, value proposition and pricing.

Example: Check the salability of the newly designed software based upon its features, value proposition, interactivity, user friendliness and pricing.

Device 3: Experience - Extreme Conditions

Check the product operations in extreme weather conditions.

This test is important to establish the quality and sustainability of the product design while using it in extreme conditions.

Test the design and product in the extreme conditions which includes heat, water and cold. Identify the weak areas which could fail the products. Modify the design so that it sustains in extreme weather conditions.

Example: The portable digital music player was tested extensively in simulated severe weather conditions for its functioning.

Device 4: Research - Legality

The design of the product should be in accordance to government's rules, laws and regulations.

The knowledge of these factors is important as slight neglect of any regulation, law or rule, while designing the product, can have acute impact on the business and life of the product.

The analysis of each and every rule, policy, regulation and law related to the product and its design need to analyzed before finalizing the product. The product design and other factors must lie within the government legal framework. The design should also be flexible enough to integrate any future changes in the rules, regulations and laws.

Example: Before finalizing the design of an IC (Internal Combustion) engine it needs to be tested for all Government rules, laws and regulations.

Device 5: Research - Assumptions

Identify all assumptions while designing the product and check them for their pragmatism.

We need to know about all of our assumptions and their sensitivities to estimate the robustness of the product design.

Check for all the assumptions we have taken for designing the product. We need to check the sensitivity of each assumption. Our objective should be to design a sustainable product for the market.

Example: Identify all assumptions while designing the new high grip truck tire.

Device 6: Research - Efficiency Analysis

This device focuses on the efficiency of navigation in a system.

The inefficiencies and blockages in the system would become evident with this device.

Identify all the activities of the system and check their efficiencies and flow of information. Check for the inadequacies and problems of the system for taking corrective actions.

Example: Designing effective navigation of a website.

Device 7: Research - Past trends Analysis

This device analyzes the past trends which have affected the design of the product.

This device would clarify the relation of market trends with the product design and would help us in future designs of the product.

List all the past trends of the market and the corresponding design of the product. Analyze the major factors which affected the design of the product over the course of evolution of the product. Understand the clear relation of the product design with the market trends. Use this relation to design products.

Example: The relation of market trends affecting the design of the computer.

Device 8: Research - Design Publications

Get ideas and insights from the worldwide design publications.

Design publications report the latest trends, ideas and developments in the product design domain. The views, information and insights from these publications would help the designers to use the latest devices and methods to design winning products.

Subscribe to the best design publications and content available in the market, which would keep the designers up-to-date with the latest ideas, technologies and insights. Designers can use this knowledge to design better products at lower cost.

Device 9: Research - Trends and Design

Establish the relation between market trends and product design.

This device helps in integrating the market trends in the design of the product.

Differentiate between long term and short term market trends which affect the product sale. It is important to notice that long term trends impacts the design of the product. Study the past trends of the market and analyze their effect on the design of the product. Create a specific relationship between trends and product design. Analyze the present market trends and modify the product design based on these powerful trends. Designers should equip themselves with an effective system to analyze the long term trends of the market and their impact on the design of the products.

Example: The ladies purse design changes with the long term trends of the market.

Device 10: Research - Visualize Future

Use forecasting methods to predict the changes in the market.

This understanding would help in creating sustainable designs of the products.

Use established forecasting methods to forecast the evolution of the product. Also, predict the future market trends. This understanding would help in integrating these factors to create a robust design of the product.

Example: Forecasting the office furniture market would help in creating a sustainable design for office tables.

Device 11: Research - Product Support

Check for the efforts required to support the product after sales.

This analysis would clarify the cost and material (e.g. spare parts etc.) required to efficiently provide the after sales support of the product.

Test the product extensively to analyze the support requirements of the product. This analysis would guide the designers by exposing the parameters which could increase the cost and complexity of after sales support. The product design can be improved to improve the efficiency and effectiveness of after sales support.

Device 12: Research - One-time Buyers

Analyze one-time buyers of related products to know their behaviors and attitudes.

This analysis would clarify the weaknesses of the existing products which are responsible for not able to attract repeat buyers. This learning can be used to create products which would have high percentage of repeat buyers.

Identify the unsuccessful products in the market which are not able to attract repeat buyers. Explore the features and design elements of these products which are responsible for their failure. Use this learning to design better products.

Example: Analysis of the failed products in the consumer durable sector gave enough learning to the designers to develop and design a successful mixer-grinder.

Device 13: Research - Product Evolution

Check for the evolution of the product line to design future products.

This analysis helps in understanding the design changes in the product and guides the designers with insights of the product evolution while explaining the reasons for the design changes in past.

Look at the history of the product and study the various designs of the past. Identify the reasons which are responsible for forcing the changes in product design. This evolution can be extrapolated to get design ideas about the product.

Example: Looking at the evolution of the design of rifle would help the designer to develop a better gun.

Device 14: Research - Manufacturing Capabilities

Check for the manufacturing capabilities required for production of the product.

This analysis would inform the designer for the capability and investment required for the production of the product. The product design can be modified to lessen the cost and complexity of product manufacturing.

Analyze the production requirements of the designed product. Check for the cost and resources required for its manufacturing. If the product development cost is over-budget then the product design needs to be changed to suit the manufacturing budget and capacities.

Example: A top class design of an electrical motor may increase the price of the product in the market, making it unsalable. The product design needs to be modified to keep the product viable and profitable.

Device 15: Research - Present Trends Analysis

It analyzes the current trends of the market, which would affect the value requirement of the product.

This device would indicate the new design requirements of the product.

Identify all the current trends of the market and industry which would affect the demand of the market. Analyze these trends to understand their impact on the usage and design of the product.

<u>Example</u>: Fashion trends affecting the dressing of the students.

Device 16: Research - Future View

Analyze the future changes in the market and the demands of the consumers.

The device is useful in keeping the designers ahead of the market demand by preparing them for drastic changes in the demands of the customers.

Use the statistical tools and forecasting methods to predict, with high confidence levels, the future of the industry and needs of target customer segments. Utilize this analysis and forecast to develop the product design plans and to allocate resources.

Example: Use forecasting methods to understand the required changes in 'Power Adapter' design for electronic devices.

Device 17: Research - Micro Analysis

This device analyzes the micro aspects of the processes and methods involved in using the product.

Micro Analysis is used to extract the hidden aspects related to product, which can affect the final design of the product.

Identify all the processes associated with the product and analyze the details of each process. Check for hidden issues and concerns which would affect the design of product. Identify the required modifications in the product design.

Example: The design of a table – fan which can be used at work and at home need to be analyzed for its usage and functioning feasibility at both the places.

Device 18: Research - Other Industries Designers

Capture the insights of the designers from other industries.

This device helps the designers by equipping them with the suggestions and ideas of other design professionals who bring in fresh perspectives.

Identify the best designers of other industries and meet them to take their suggestions and views about the design of your products. These people would bring in new ideas and perspectives which could help the designers in creating a better product.

Example: To design a new washing machine the suggestions from the designers of television sets, home interior and computers may be useful.

Device 19: Research - Relationships study

Use this device to find the relationship between various elements of the products and their environments.

This device is useful in looking for opportunities in the relationships existing in the environment of the product. These insights would give us new ideas about improving the design of the product.

Understand the environment of the product in detail and identify the various relationships in it. Draw the relationship diagram between these elements. Look for the missing aspects and potential issues to generate new design ideas. Integrate the identified facts in the design of the product.

Example: To design a new electric generator, look for the various environments in which it would be used to check hidden issues and innovation opportunities.

Device 20: Research - Physical Attributes Analysis

For a new market check for the physical aspects feasibility of the target users of the product.

This device helps in modifying or creating the products to suit the physical aspects of the target population.

Use secondary data to analyze the physical attributes of the target population which would include physical aspects like height, weight, size of limbs etc. The product should be designed keeping these aspects in mind and tested thoroughly in the target market. It is important to note that for any new market this analysis and test has to be conducted to launch suitable products in the market.

Example: The size of shoes used by Asian and American customers would be different as the foot size of Asian customers is smaller.

Device 21: Research - Demographic Study

Study the demographic factors of the targeted population.

This study is important to establish the impact of demographics factors like gender, age, income, and education etc. of the target customers on the product design.

Check demographic data from private and public sources to analyze the required aspects of the targeted area. Check for the impact of these factors on the design on the products currently being used by them. Integrate these factors in the design of the new product.

Example: The design of kitchen wares would differ based upon demographic factors.

Device 22: Research - Psychographic Study

Study the Psychographic factors of the targeted population.

This study is important to establish the impact of psychographic like social classes, interests, activities, attitudes and lifestyle etc. of the target customers on the product design.

Check psychographic data from private and public sources to analyze the relevant factors of the targeted area. Check for the impact of these factors on the design on the products being used by them. Integrate these factors in the design of the product.

Example: The design of social clubs would differ based upon psychographic factors.

Device 23: Research - Repeat Buyers

Analyze repeat buyers to know their behaviors and attitudes.

This analysis would clarify the strength of the existing products which have dedicated repeat buyers. This learning can be used to create products which would have high percentage of repeat buyers.

Identify the successful products in the market with high percentage of repeat buyers. Explore the features and design elements of these products which make them attractive and exclusive. Use this learning to design sticky products.

Example: Analysis of the popular products in the consumer durable sector gave enough learning to the designers to develop and design a successful mixer-grinder.

Device 24: Research - Secondary Research

Collect and analyze all the published data and information about target market.

Secondary research gives the designers the various perspectives and extensive historical data to analyze the market.

Check for all the appropriate published data by private and public sources to analyze the various aspects of the targeted population.

Example: The design of houses at a location requires extensive secondary research to understand the various factors which are required to be considered.

Device 25: Research - Behavioral Study

Segmenting the potential customers based upon their behaviors and personalities.

It is important as segmenting would clarify the communication methodology to various segments of the customer group. Each customer segment would act as a niche and the value proposition of the product and its design aspects can be communicated in the effective way to each type of customers, for maximum impact.

Analyze your target population and identify various personality and behavioral parameters grouping the customers. Segment them based upon their personalities, behaviors and lifestyles. Identify the impactful communication strategy for each segment.

Example: A restaurant can offer various meal packs for different customer segments.

Device 26: Research - Competitive Analysis

Analyze the competitors of the product and company in the market.

This device is helpful in creating benchmarks for product and its design. This analysis also clarifies the main ideas and competencies of competitors about the product research and development.

Collect all required data and information about the competitors and competing products in the market. Analyze this data for creating performance standards, benchmarks and value propositions.

Example: To design a new television set, analyzing the product features, value propositions and designs of all top products is necessary.

Device 27: Research - Cultural Differences

Analyze the differences in cultures at various places.

This device is helpful in understanding and appreciating the differences in cultures and designing or modifying the product accordingly.

Use available information & data to analyze and understand the culture of the targeted area and population for which the product is to be designed. It is also important to check cultural differences from other locations, where the product could be used in future. The product design decision should be taken based upon these differences.

Example: The design of the water container may differ in various cultures and places.

Device 28: Research - Other Markets

Study other markets for similar products and customers to get new learning, knowledge and ideas.

This understanding would help the designers to get the ideas about the existing product designs in use and their limitations, weaknesses and strengths. They can use this information to design a more suitable and better product.

Identify all the markets with similar needs and requirements and the products currently used in these markets. Analyze these products in detail for all required aspects. Incorporate these insights in the new design of the products.

Example: To design an inexpensive car, evaluate the cars being used in third world countries.

Device 29: Research - Third Person Analysis

The designer analyzes the product and its design as a third person, not connected to the project in any way.

This is useful in getting an unbiased and fresh view about the product.

Third person is an independent person and in no way related to any of the stakeholders of the company. Ask your designers to consider themselves as a third person for their product and analyze it critically as an outsider.

Example: To improve the product design the designers formed a multidimensional team to analyze their toys for kids in the market.

Device 30: Research - Product Disposal

Check for various practical ways to dispose the product by users after its effective usable life.

This analysis is important for finalizing the material to be used for developing the product, which can be easily disposed by the end-user.

Analyze the government regulations regarding the waste disposal. It is important to note that the disposed material needs to be environment friendly, recyclable and easy to dispose. Based upon this analysis decide on the materials and components to be used for developing the product based upon product design.

Example: The material to develop the soft-drink cans should be in accordance to the government rules and regulations.

Device 31: Research - Customer Delight

Check for the various features and design aspect of the product which would delight the consumers.

This device helps in understanding the thinking process of end-users better by understanding their emotional connection with the product.

Collect the information and insights available in the market about the various features and design aspects of the products which are appreciated by the customers. These ideas can be analyzed for their integration in the product design.

Example: To develop a new furniture range the designers analyzed the existing furnitures available in the market for design & materials used and to answer the question "Why is it successful?"

Device 32: Research - Customer Dislikes

Check for the various features and design aspects of the related products, which are unpopular in the market.

This analysis would help the designers by warning them for the features and design aspects, which would be disliked by the end-users.

Collect the information and insights available in the market about the various features and design aspects of the products which are unpopular. These insights can be analyzed to understand the thinking process of customers and their dislikes.

Example: To develop a new furniture range the designers analyzed the existing furnitures available in the market for design & materials used and to answer the questions "Why it failed in the market?"

Device 33: Research - Need Ring

Need Ring pre-warns the designers about the future changes in the market.

This device is useful in anticipating and designing new products much before they would be demanded in the market.

This concept is based upon the concept of need and demand. Need is the requirements of the market but all is not demanded by the consumers. Demand is the smaller circle inside the need circle. Demand is the immediate requirement of the market. This means that some portion of the need is not yet demanded. If we could create a thin ring above the demand circle, it becomes the 'Need Ring'. This ring consists of the requirements of the market, which are not yet demanded, but would soon be demanded. The marketers and designers need to analyze this ring. The current trends and macro factors of the market would help in analyzing the constituents of the need ring. Designers need to develop products for this ring as these products would soon be demanded in the market.

<u>Example</u>: Steve Jobs was the master in identifying the need rings in the market and developing the quality products which would be embraced by the market.

Device 34: Research - Design Attraction

Understand the design features which pull the people to buy the products in the market.

This analysis would give deeper understanding to the designers about the design features which would be valued by the consumers.

Identify the successful products in the market and check for consumer feedback about the respected design aspects of these products. Capture all the valued design elements and ideas of the chosen products. This understanding would be useful for designing the new products for the market.

Example: To design a new office table check for all the successful furniture ranges in the market and understand their unique design aspects.

Device 35: Research - Customer Financials

Understand the financial strength of the customer segment so as to design product which suits their budget and expenditure.

This device is helpful in designing products which would be bought in the market.

Identify the target customer segment in the market. Get the data and information about the budgeting, savings and expenditures of the targeted niche. This information is important in designing the products with pricing well within the budget of the customers.

Example: To design the scooter for young ladies would require understanding the spending capacity of this customer segment.

Device 36: Research - Other Values

Identify the other values the product adds to the customer e.g. reputation, glamour.

This understanding is useful in knowing the impact of product design in the life of users, which would guide designers to design better products.

Collect secondary data and conduct primary research to analyze the value additions of the product in the life of the people. Primary surveys, with closed ended questions, can be conducted to understand these values. These surveys would also disclose the role of product design in specified value addition.

Example: A high end watch with great design and strong brand adds value to the customer by providing accurate time and status.

Device 37: Research - Perceptions

Note the various perceptions of the various users about the existing products in the market.

This analysis is useful in getting the complete spectrum of the perceptions existing in the market about the products used by consumers.

Identify products to be analyzed in the market. Check for the various types of the customers in the market, including the extreme users. Note the perceptions of these users and the reasons associated with their specific views. Use this insight in designing the products which would cater to the complete range of users.

Example: To design a new motor-cycle the market needs to be analyzed for the various perceptions about the existing two-wheelers in the market.

Device 38: Research - Product Material

Check for the material which would be used by the product.

This analysis helps in checking for a range of materials which could be used to develop the product.

Based upon the usage of the product the material needs to be decided by the designer, for product development. Before finalization, different materials need to be short-listed and tested for the various performance parameters of the product. The material to be finalized would be most optimized for development and usage.

Example: To design a remote control for television various materials needs to be analyzed for robustness and durability.

Device 39: Research - Other Industries Marketers

Capture the insights of the marketers from other industries.

This device helps the designer by equipping them with the suggestions and ideas of other professionals who brings in fresh perspectives.

Identify the best marketers of other industries and meet them to take their suggestions and views about the market and the design of your products. These people would bring in new ideas and viewpoints which could help the designers in creating a better product.

Example: To design a new washing machine the suggestions from the marketers of television sets, home interior and computers may be useful.

Device 40: Research - Profitability Analysis

Check the long term profitability of the product and forecast it for long term.

This analysis establishes the business case for the product. If the product is not profitable then the product needs to be optimized with design changes.

Analyze the cost for manufacturing the product. Forecast the pricing, revenues and profitability of the product. Is the product a viable proposition? If not, the required changes need to be made to the product to build a logical case for its development.

Example: The design of a car model was modified to adjust it within the cost and price range.

Device 41: Research - Feasibility Study

Study the feasibility of developing the designed product.

This study clarifies the feasibility of developing the product. If the product is not realistic to develop then its design has to be changed or it should be scrapped.

Conduct the feasibility of the product looking at all the aspects from procuring the raw material till the final delivery of the product. Any problem related to the feasibility of the product needs to be undertaken immediately.

Example: New sealed packages were designed to protect the perishable food items.

Device 42: Research - Macro Analysis

Analyze the product and its positioning on the macro platform.

This is a nice way to have the big-picture view of the product.

Create the charts of the sector and industry and position the product on those charts. Similarly analyze the customer segment served with this product.

Example: A new washing machine design was analyzed for its positioning in the consumer durable industry and electronic products.

EXPERIENCE SEGMENT

This segment of READ modal consists of devices which emphasize on the importance of experiencing the product, which would be used by the consumers. These devices reveal hidden areas which are difficult to discuss or observe.

Device 43: Experience - In Other's Shoes

Experience the feelings of the user, while consuming or using the product or service.

The designer needs to understand the problems and limitations of the special conditions of the consumers for designing the product.

The designers can wear ear plugs or heavy clothing to simulate the limitations of the end-users. These experiences are important to understand the conditions of the users so as to design a right product for the consumers.

Example: While designing the chair for heavy and bulky people the designers wore special clothing and put on extra weight to simulate the experience of the user.

Device 44: Experience - Extreme Usage

Check for extreme users and their various ways which can cause product to fail.

This analysis helps in understanding the extreme usage of the product and in identifying the design modifications which could protect the product from breaking down.

Identify the extreme users of the product and check for the eccentric ways the product could be used. Considering these users as the future consumers of the product modify the design to safeguard the product from failing.

Example: To design a new ball-point pen the team of designers analyzed all the users, especially extreme users, to develop a robust design of the product.

Device 45: Experience - Use as Consumer

Use the product with the consumers at their locations.

This is useful to understand, observe and experience the product usage at the right location, revealing unknown problems and contexts.

Use the designed product at the location of customer and use it in various ways, which could be decent or aggressive. Notify the experiences, feelings and observations while using the product.

Example: Designers used oral care product at consumer's home, exactly in the real conditions in which the product would be used, to understand product's positive and negative points.

Device 46: Experience - Design Touching Senses

Check for the human senses which would be touched by the product design.

This understanding would help in refining the product design by making it soothing and gratifying for human senses.

Observe and analyze the various ways in which the product design would touch the five human senses of the consumers. Understand its effect on the consumer's feelings and emotions. The design of the product must be pleasurable for the consumers to use.

Example: The design of the ladies purse was tested for its pleasurable effect on the human senses.

Device 47: Experience - Robustness

Check the robustness of the product by ageing it.

This is helpful in understanding and estimating the life of the product.

Use various methods to age the product and test its robustness and quality. Find the weak areas which can affect the age of the product negatively, so as to modify the design accordingly.

Example: The readymade garments were tested for quality and durability by speed aging them in various conditions.

Device 48: Experience - Extreme Environment and Climates

Check the product operations in extreme environments and climates.

This test is important to establish the quality and sustainability of the product design while using it internationally in various environments and climates.

Test the design and product at numerous places which includes different environments and climates. Identify the weak areas which could fail the products. Modify the design so that it sustains in extreme weather conditions.

Example: The portable digital music player is tested extensively in simulated severe environments and climates for its functioning.

Device 49: Experience - Training to Use the Product

Check for ease of use of the product. Is any training required to use the product?

This understanding is useful in keeping simplicity at the center of the design of the product.

Distribute the prototype of the product to various users, from layman to experts, and let them understand the use the product, themselves, without any support, training or guidance. Observe their experience and behavior to identify the design changes required in the product for simplifying its usage.

Example: The newly developed office utility software was tested with various executives to check for its user friendly interface.

Device 50: Experience - Create Working Model

The designers should create the working model of the design concept of the product.

These working models are important for the evaluation of the concept and helps in revealing the hidden issues and problems, which need attention of the designers. These concepts and working models need to be iterated till a proper working model is evolved.

Note down all the finalized concepts of the product and develop the working model for each idea. These models need to be tested by designers in various ways to reveal the weaknesses of the idea. The required idea needs to be modified for correction and the model should be developed again for testing. This process needs to be repeated till the final working and satisfactory design concept is ready.

Example: The design concept of the mobile phone needs to be iterated and the working models tested extensively to finalize the design of the mobile phone.

Device 51: Experience - New Environment

With proposed future environment and design, get the experience as a consumer.

This is helpful in experiencing the proposed design by the designers.

To test the viability and effectiveness of the proposed design the product is tested and experienced in the actual environment and situations.

Example: Checking the new design of the packaged food pack in actual environment and circumstances of office and restaurants.

Device 52: Experience - Interaction Design

Use two dimensional images and designs for testing them for human interactions.

This type of testing is fast and economical to check the design of interfaces.

Use pictures or draw the interfaces on paper or screen to be checked by designers and end users. The experience of using the interfaces would reveal the hidden aspects and problems in the interaction design of the interface. This process can be repeated to optimize the design of the interface.

Example: To design the interface of a software application of touch screen tablet device would involve several interfaces designed on paper or charts and consumers use them to check the usage experience. The interaction design would be refined with each iteration.

Device 53: Experience - Look into the Future

Let the multifunctional team of the company define the future for their company within the forecasted environment.

This forecast is useful in designing the product which would have long term relevance.

Organize a multifunctional meeting to forecast about the future environment, market and industry. Also, discuss about the changes in the company and its products offering due to these forecasts. The product design needs to suit these forecasts. It is important to note that the design needs to be flexible enough to create the required changes in the product if required.

Example: Designing the refrigerator based upon the forecasts of the company.

Device 54: Experience - Feel it physically

Setup scenarios and play roles for various users, focusing on the instinctive responses prompted by the physical enactment of the role or situation.

This is useful in testing ideas in various contexts and understanding behavior based responses of the consumers.

<u>Example</u>: The interiors of a long route train were designed by actually creating and enacting various scenarios to create maximum comfort for the travelers.

Device 55: Experience - Basic Model

Use basic materials like thermocole, paper and color to create basic models of the product.

Using basic models the team can visualize the product to be designed.

During the initial process of designing the product use the basic things like paper, thermocole, color and other material to create a fast physical model of the product. These models give a physical feel to the product and its looks and size can be analyzed. These basic models graduate to the working models of the product.

Example: While designing a set-top-box several basic models were created before developing the working model of the product.

Device 56: Experience - On Stage

Let the designers play the role of each user of the product during an event.

This device is used to get the real life experience of the product or requirement during an activity for which the product is to be developed.

Identify various events related to the product and let each designer play the role of the users of the product. Let them note their experiences on a journal, which can be used to refine the design of the product.

Example: Designers played a company board meeting to design the presentation devices used in the meeting.

Device 57: Experience - Usage Models

Use the prototype of the product to check it in various environments and spaces.

This helps in understanding the deficiencies and problems in the prototype of the product.

Develop the working prototype of the product and use it in various ways and settings. The objective is to find any weaknesses in the design of the product, which can be corrected.

<u>Example</u>: Check the prototype of the shoe in various conditions for performance parameters.

Device 58: Experience - Various Users Testing

Check the product with various users.

Different consumers use the product in various ways which can illuminate the designers about any hidden problems with design of the product.

Identify the various users of the product and ask them to use the prototype of the product in various ways. Check for the deficiencies in the product.

<u>Example</u>: Check the design of the television remote control with various users.

Device 59: Experience - Usage Stories

Create visual stories of using the product in various ways and let the potential consumers comment on it for gaps.

This device helps in improving the features of the product, while explaining the value of each feature.

Create videos and pictures of the various events when the product would be used and ask future users to share their views.

Example: Create video stories of using a new design of carrying bag in various circumstances and ask users to comment on these stories.

Device 60: Experience - Use it

Let designers use the new designed product.

Using the products designed by them the designers have the experience of the end users of the product and they will be able to innovate better.

Ask the designers to use the first prototype of the product for substantial time to find problems with the design.

Example: Designers used the first prototype of the office briefcase for one week to check for the expected value addition.

Device 61: Experience - Product Assembling

Check for any requirement of assembling of the product before using it.

This analysis is useful to understand the ease of using the product by the customer, just after opening the brand new pack of the product.

Test with various categories of consumers about opening the protection packing of the product and the simplicity in assembling the product to use it immediately. The assembling should to be 'no-brainer' which means that it should be easy to assemble, even for a layman to use the product, without any help or support.

Example: The new laptop is tested for its ease of assembling and immediate usage by the consumers.

Device 62: Experience - Limitations

Check for the limitations for using the product.

This is important to clarify the expectations of the consumers from the product.

The product should be tested with minimum and maximum parameters to check for its limitations.

<u>Example</u>: The refrigerator design was tested for the minimum and maximum voltages on which it can operate.

Device 63: Experience - Live With Them

Designers live with the various consumers like their family members to understand them better.

This method is extremely useful to understand the attitudes, behaviors, emotions and feeling of the consumers.

Choose consumers from various categories of the customer segments and stay with them as their family members while regularly taking text, audio, video and picture notes to understand their thinking, psychology and decisions. Analyze these notes to design a suitable product for them.

Example: To design a family car the designers stayed with the potential customer's families to understand their unspecified requirements.

Device 64: Experience - Product Packaging

Analyze the design of the product packaging which could keep it safe and is good for the environment.

The analysis of product packaging is important as it keeps the product safe and creates the first impression in the mind of the buyer.

Create various packaging of the product and test it in various conditions to check its robustness, ease of opening and other safety parameters. Also, check it for its attraction and looks.

Example: The packaging of the mixer grinder was tested thoroughly for its strength, safety and ease of opening.

Device 65: Experience - Precautions

Check for the precautions for using the product.

This analysis is extremely important to keep the safety of the users into consideration.

Identify all the ways in which the product can affect the user negatively. The design of the product should take into consideration all these aspects. Precautions to use the product should be specified clearly on the product and its packaging, as even a safe product requires precautions to use it.

Example: A television set, which is generally safe, has certain precautions to use it.

Device 66: Experience - Existing Users

Analyze the existing users using the similar products.

This process acquaints the designers with various ways the product would be used.

Identify a set of similar products available in the market. Analyze the regular users of these products and note the various ways the product is being used by them.

Example: To design a new office chair the team of designers visited various offices and analyzed the existing office chairs in use.

Device 67: Experience - Product Integration

Check for various ways the product gets integrated in consumer's life.

Let users record with pictures, videos and written facts about the various ways the product gets embedded in the user's life.

Give users cameras and ask them to record the use of the product by capturing pictures and videos.

<u>Example</u>: Consumers were asked to capture the use of office bag through pictures and videos.

Device 68: Experience - Designer Perception

Check for the perception of designers about the customer experiences.

This is useful to contrast the perceived and actual experiences and feelings of the customers.

Record the actual experiences of the customers while using the products. Use pictures, audios, videos and descriptions to record these consumer's experiences. Ask the designers to describe in detail the experiences and emotional states of the customers while using the products. Present the gap in the understanding of the designers.

Example: Designers were asked to explain their understanding about the usage of new Microwave. Gaps in their understanding were presented to them by showing them the videos of actual usage of the product.

ANALYZE SEGMENT

This segment of READ model focuses on different ways the consumers are analyzed through observations and recording. The devices in Analyze segment aims to understand the problem areas and innovation opportunities through studying their actions and behaviors.

Device 69: Analyze - Invisible Presence

Record and analyze the actions and behaviors of the end-users while performing the activity without disturbing them in any way.

This analysis helps in getting the clarity about the actual activities performed by the users in real time, which is much better than asking them about describing their actions.

Identify the activities related to the product and observe people performing them. The presence of the designers needs to be invisible which means that they observe the actions performed by the people without interfering them in any way.

Example: Designers observed and analyzed the sales professionals giving sales presentations to understand the need for a suitable product for presentation.

Device 70: Analyze - Other Product's Usage

Check for the ways the other products are used by the consumers.

This analysis helps in giving information about the various ways the product would be used.

Identify the products to be analyzed for usage. Observe and record the consumers using those products. This analysis specifies the various ways the product could fail and other factors which can improve the product design.

Example: To design an office chair the designers analyzed the usage of furniture and other related product by the consumers.

Device 71: Analyze - Buying Behavior in Stores

Record and analyze the buying behavior of the consumers to understand their thinking process during buying the products.

This analysis helps in clarifying the visual design parameters which attracts and motivates the consumers to buy.

Use video cameras at strategic locations at department stores and shops to observe people while they make the buying decisions. Analyze this data to understand the decision making process of consumers to buy the products.

Example: Installation of video cameras in a toy store clarified the designers about the visual parameters which impacts the buying decisions of the customers.

Device 72: Analyze - New Product and Life

Check the various ways in which the designed product gets integrated with the life of the consumers.

This information is useful by clarifying the future uses of the product.

Distribute the product prototypes of the designed product to the participants and analyze the various ways the product would be used by the consumers. Check for value of the product in the life of the consumers and various ways the product gets integrated into the life of the consumer.

Example: Analyze the various ways in which a new smartphone design gets integrated into the life of the consumer and its value delivery.

Device 73: Analyze - Carrying the Product

Check for the various ways the product would be carried by the potential customers.

This observation would the helpful in creating a design of the product that it is safe and easier to carry.

Identify the different ways the similar products are carried. Distribute the prototype of the product to the potential consumers and ask them to naturally place and carry the product in various ways.

Example: To refine the design of the office bag the users were observed for several days for the various ways the bag was used and carried.

Device 74: Analyze - Product failing

Check for various ways when the product would fail during its usage.

This understanding would compel the designers to improve the product design to make it more robust.

Ask the participants to use the product naturally and observe the various events when the product would fail. These events and failures should be analyzed to improve the product design.

Example: The prototypes of a new wristwatch were distributed to the participants and were asked to behave naturally and perform actions of their daily life which could affect the product maximum. Observe and record these events and analyze them to improve the product design.

Device 75: Analyze - Visual Affects

Check how the visuals of the product affect the buying decisions of the product.

This analysis would help in improving the looks of the product so as to make it more attractive.

Use various shapes and color scheme of the product to check for its attractiveness. Finalize the shapes and color schemes of the product which affects the visual attraction of the product.

Example: The color and design of the pencil-box was finalized after certain review of the product.

Device 76: Analyze - Innovative Usage of Product

Check for various ways the product would be used by consumers.

This analysis is helpful in creating the design of the product which would satisfy various users.

Distribute the prototype of the product to various categories of users and observe them over a period of time for different ways the product is used by consumers.

Example: The new design of carry bag was tested for its different uses.

Device 77: Analyze - Capture Pictures

Capture the pictures of objects and people doing certain activities related to the design project.

This device helps in identifying the patterns of behaviors of consumers during certain activities.

Capture the photographs of people during specific time performing certain activities to understand their habits and behavioral patterns.

Example: Designers captured pictures of people cooking food to understand various patterns for designing the product to improve their efficiency.

Device 78: Analyze - Project Visits

Escort the consumers on the product design related visits and observe their experiences and thinking.

This is useful in notifying the feelings and experiences of the participants in real time. This exercise would produce the effective information and insights which cannot be generated during simple interview.

Take consumer's permission to accompany them on relevant visits, which are related to product design. Observe, notify and capture the real-time ideas, observations and thinking of the participants.

Example: Designers accompanied the shoppers in the department store to look for ways to improve their shopping experience.

Device 79: Analyze - Daily Objects

Identify the objects which the potential consumers interacts with every day.

This observation generates insights about the objects with which the designed product would interact every day. This understanding would help the designer to design better protection and ease of usage of the product.

Interact with the end-users of the product to understand the objects they use and interact with every day. Also, check the various ways these products are used and carried, and the effect they could have on the designed product.

Example: To design a female smart-phone the designers checked for the objects with which the potential consumers interact with every day and the various ways the phone would be carried.

Device 80: Analyze - Become their Friend

Visit and spend time with the users during the specific usage time of the product.

This exercise helps the designer to observe the consumers using the product in real time, over a period of time.

Check for the specific usage time of the product by the consumer and visit them for several days to observe its usage by them.

Example: Designers observed the usage of the instrument to check blood pressure every day, for one week.

Device 81: Analyze - Product and Life

Check the various ways in which the existing product gets integrated with the life of the consumers.

This information is useful by clarifying the future uses of the product.

Follow the consumers for few days and collect information about the product usage at various intervals. Analyze the value propositions of the product in the life of customers. Prepare detailed uses of the product.

Example: Analyze the various ways in which a smartphone gets integrated into the life of the consumer and its value delivery.

Device 82: Analyze - Body Double

Accompany potential users to understand their routine and interactions.

This is a powerful way to reveal design opportunities and show how a product might affect or complement user's behaviors and actions.

Move with potential users to observe and understand their day-to-day routines, interactions and contexts.

Example: Designers accompanied the school kids to design a better school-bag for them.

Device 83: Analyze - Social Connections

Identify the various relationships, connections and flow of information between a group and network.

This is useful in understanding the official, casual and interpersonal relationships between networks and smaller groups and the flow of information between them.

Create 2D or 3D diagrams and models to capture the social connections between the groups and networks.

Example: Social connection analysis helped a big organization to improve the communication between its various departments and regions.

Device 84: Analyze - Problems from Product

Find the various ways the product can create the problems for consumers.

This analysis is important to understand the product aspects which need to be avoided.

Designers should test the product extensively in various conditions, places and circumstances for possible problems which can be caused with the usage of the product.

Example: The new batteries were tested extensively, in all possible conditions, for their heating or bursting.

Device 85: Analyze - Supporting Product or Service

Check for the supporting product or service required to use the designed product.

This analysis would be helpful in creating a solution for the market.

Analyze the various ways the designed product would be used by different categories of customers. Check for the supporting product or service which would be required to use it.

Example: A smartphone would require operating system, applications, SIM card and internet connection to operate.

Device 86: Analyze - How They Live?

Observe the consumers when they live in the house.

This observation would reveal hidden opportunities for innovation.

Put video cameras in the people's home at relevant place and record their daily activities. This observation may open up the possibilities of developing products which could make their life better and productive.

Example: An opportunity for preparing meals faster was found by observing their time spend in kitchen.

Device 87: Analyze - All Categories of Customers

Analyze the product design for its suitability for all categories of customers.

The analysis is important in expanding the size of the market.

Divide the target customer segment into various categories. Analyze and test the product design suiting the requirements of all categories.

Example: A laptop design should suit the requirements of all categories of customers.

Device 88: Analyze - Consumer's Habits

Understand and record the habits of the consumers.

This is helpful in creating products which would get better integrated into their lives.

Observe the potential consumers performing tasks in context of the product design and observe the habits and behaviors. The designers should consider these facts in the product design which would better integrate the product in people's life.

Example: To design sofa-set, designers looked for various ways the sofa would be used by people.

Device 89: Analyze - Video Capture

Use video cameras to record movements of people and objects in a space over a prolonged period of time.

This is useful in providing a macro view of the space within the context of the project.

Finalize the space to be analyzed for a design project and put video cameras (infra-red enabled) to record every movement in the space over a large period of time. These videos can be speed viewed to understand the usage of space.

Example: The reception area of a big company was observed for several weeks to redesign it for better usage.

Device 90: Analyze - Consumer Day

Spend a day with consumer to understand their experiences and feelings.

This is important to check for unexpected issues and problems which the consumers experience every day.

Accompany a consumer for the whole day, without interfering them in any way, and notify your observations of their experiences and problems they face. This exercise can provide opportunities for innovation.

Example: A cosmetic company conducted analysis of ladies traveling during summers to develop a skin care product.

Device 91: Analyze - Personal Productivity

Observe people at work and check for their various habits which make them more productive.

This exercise would act like an idea bank as each observation would give designers a new idea for personal productivity.

Observe the large number of people during their work time and notify minutely the specific actions which make them productive and efficient. This exercise is especially effective while observing them meeting their deadlines or completing the urgent work.

Exercise: The observation of the 100 sales managers over three months gave wealth of insights about the new ways to store important information using pen and paper.

Device 92: Analyze - Movement Patterns

Observe and notify the usage of a space by people over a period of time.

These observations help the designers to analyze the usage of a space and specific behavioral patterns.

Divide the space to be analyzed into several equal segments and observe its usage over a period of time to notify its usage by people. Designers can identify several patterns of the people while using the space.

Example: Designers observed a train platform for its usage to analyze the movement patterns of the commuters.

DISCOVER SEGMENT

Discover segment of READ model includes devices which focuses on the various ways the designers interact directly with the consumers to understand their views, requirements, desires and perceptions.

Device 93: Discover - Segmented Users Testing

Segment the users and test each of them, in detail, to get their views about the product.

This analysis would give designers various ideas and hidden problems related to the product.

Segment the users of the product or service and test the product or product model with all types of categories. Let them openly comment, give suggestions and share experiences about the product. This process need to be repeated till each segment looks satisfied with the product.

Example: The control panel of an electronic device was tested with various segments of users to refine its design.

Device 94: Discover - Customer's Dislikes

Understand the dislikes of the customer in the existing products, so that designers could be careful in future designs.

This understanding cautions the designers about the aspects and features they need to avoid in the design.

Identify the similar products existing in the market and survey the consumers for the characteristics of the product which are detested by them. Also, check for the reasons for the specified dislikes. This information can be used to design better products which would be liked by the market, even by the fierce critics.

Example: To design a new Personal Computer (PC), the market was scanned for the areas which are disliked by the consumers in existing PCs.

Device 95: Discover - Ask for Features

Ask the potential consumers about the features which they would like to have in the product.

This analysis creates a list of features which are desired by the consumers.

Conduct an extensive survey covering all the categories of the customers to understand their requirements and expectations of the features. All these features can be listed to create a final feature list for the product design.

Example: To design a new mobile phone the market was surveyed for the features which the consumers would 'Love to have' and 'must have'.

Device 96: Discover - Feature Priorities

Ask the potential consumers about the priority of features they would like to have in the product.

This analysis helps in finalizing the list of features which would be included in the final product.

Compile the list of product features which would be desired by the market. Conduct an extensive survey covering all the categories of the customers to understand their requirements and priority of the specified features. The final list of features can be made from priority listing of features.

Example: To design a new mobile phone the market was surveyed for the priority of features in the product.

Device 97: Discover - Customer Journal

Ask the consumers to create a journal of their day with pictures, audio, videos and descriptions.

This journal would help the designers to understand their customers better.

Create a 'Daily Journal Kit' for the consumers, which would help them to record their day with text, photos, audios and videos. Ask the participants to record their day with descriptions. This recording needs to be general and not specific to any specific task or act. These journals can be analyzed for deepening their understanding the customer segment, which would help designers to create emphatic products.

Example: A design company keeps collecting the customer journals to use them as their competitive advantage in designing successful products.

Device 98: Discover - Customer Feedback

Check the customer feedback for the existing products.

This survey is helpful in understanding the views of the customers about the products in the market, which could help the designers to integrate the positive feedback and learn from the negative feedback to improve their product designs. These surveys can be macro or on any specific micro level.

Identify the popular but similar products in the market and conduct and extensive feedback analysis. This analysis can also be available in the market as a secondary research. Understand the perceptions, experiences and feelings about these products.

Example: Before designing a new washing machine the designers conducted the extensive feedback research for washing machines present in the market and other consumer durable products.

Device 99: Discover - Product Value

How do consumers value the product in their life?

This analysis is helpful in knowing the value proposition of the product and features responsible for delivering this value.

Interact with a set of consumers to understand the value addition by the product in their lives. Check for the features responsible for this value addition. Design the product to enhance the value proposition of the product.

Example: The value proposition of the basic mobile phone was analyzed to understand its utility value. New features were added to the phone to enhance its value like mobile torch.

Device 100: Discover - Cross Question

Question the consumers repeatedly to understand the fundamental reasons for using a product.

This information is helpful in understanding their behaviors, decisions and attitudes in context of a product.

Prepare a large list of questions and cross questions to make the consumer reveal the underlying reason for their decisions and actions. The set of cross questions would help the designers to dig deeper into their psyche and understand them better.

Example: Designers used cross questions to understand the actual reasons of consumers to use a specific brand of cosmetics.

Device 101: Discover - Conceptualize

Use images to develop and explain a concept

This exercise is used to understand the ideas and perceptions of issues and helps them to specify complex or unexplainable themes.

To understands the consumer's perception about the evolution of new technology the participants were asked to conceptualize their perception by using pictures and other visuals.

Device 102: Discover - Other Markets

Understand and analyze the products used in other markets including international markets.

This information would help the designers to understand international design principles and standards.

Identify the international markets and the products to be analyzed and conduct a cross-cultural study to understand the general and specific international design principles. This would help the designers to study the usage of the products in the various environments and contexts in which the products are used.

Example: Analysis of oral care products gave the designers new insights about the products to be designed.

Device 103: Discover - Think Aloud

Ask the consumers to speak their thinking while performing some specific activities.

This is an effective way to understand their ideas, thinking, perceptions, motivations and reasons.

Identify the tasks in the context of the design project and meet consumers while performing those tasks. Ask them to speak out all of their thinking while performing the task. The designers need to record these and analyze these points to understand them in relation to the product design.

Example: Asking people to think aloud while preparing breakfast gave designers the idea about developing nutritious food with minimal amount of time to prepare.

Device 104: Discover - Interviewing

Interview consumers to understand their ideas and perceptions.

This exercise helps in getting the views from a large number of people about a specific area in least amount of time.

Prepare a set of open-ended and closed-ended questions to survey a sample of target segment. The answers can be collected in controlled situations. These answers reveal certain ideas, perceptions and views about the consumers.

Example: Interviewing helped designers to understand the modifications required in the recently launched educational product in the market.

Device 105: Discover - Focus Groups

Ask various categories of potential customers to discuss and share ideas about the product.

This discussion raises various points and generates ideas and expectations of customers about the new product, features and its design.

For a certain product idea categorize the target customers into various segments. Conduct product discussion meetings with these potential customers. These meetings can be conducted into various formats ranging from category-wise to mixed teams. These ideas and views can be recorded, which can be analyzed to finalize the design parameters of the product.

Example: To design a new medium-range smartphone, several dedicated and mixed meetings were conducted with the potential customers to get ideas about its features, size and pricing.

Device 106: Discover - Word Design

Check how consumers associate words with specific design concepts and features.

This exercise helps to prioritize the design concepts and features of the product to be designed.

Ask participants to associate expressive words with diverse design concepts or features in order to show how they perceive and value the issues.

Example: To design a table fan participants were asked to choose and prioritize the design aspects of the product.

Device 107: Discover - Requirement Analysis

Document and analyze the requirements of the consumers.

This analysis clarifies the demand of the market.

Discuss the proposed product with the potential consumers and understand their demands and desires. Analyze them to finalize the feature-set of the product to be designed.

Example: To design a new organizer and planner the market was scanned for the new requirements of the customers and the price they are ready to pay for the enhanced product.

Device 108: Discover - Meet Critics

Meet the biggest product design critics and understand their views.

This analysis would bring in fresh professional views, which can be integrated with other insights to design the product.

Identify the major product critics in the market and meet them for their views about a great product. Check for your learning from the discussions and use these insights to improve the product design.

Example: The views and suggestions of the movie critics were used to create a next successful film by a Hollywood movie director.

Device 109: Discover - Other Markets

Get the views and experiences of the customers from other markets.

This analysis gives new perspective to the design of the product of the consumers from other cultures and demographics.

Identify the relevant markets for analysis and conduct a survey to understand their views about the product design and features.

Example: To design a new office table, other consumers were also consulted for their views on the good design of an office table.

Device 110: Discover - Buying Thinking Process

Understand the buying thinking process of the consumers.

This analysis is helpful in clarifying the aspects of the product which make the customer to decide on buying the product.

The experts in the consumer psychology can help in understanding the buying thinking process of the consumers. This understanding would help the designers to integrate the required features and aspects which would support in increasing the sale of the product.

Example: To design a better packaging of washing powder the consumers were observed and analyzed at various retail stores.

Device 111: Discover - Perceptions

Check for various perceptions about the product.

This analysis is important to understand perception of the product to predict the future usage of the product.

Meet people from various customer segments to understand the various perceptions they have about the product and the various ways it could add value.

Example: Look for the various perceptions about a container

Device 112: Discover - Picture Book

Motivate the participants to record their views and experiences on a notebook, in expressive format.

This device exposes the hidden point of views and expectations of the customers.

Ask participants to prepare a picture book, which includes pictures and descriptions, about their impressions, circumstances, and activities related to the product.

Example: Participants were asked to record their experiences with new digital camera on a pleasure trip to a beach.

Device 113: Discover - Card Organization

Ask participants to organize cards in the most logical and suitable order, to understand their mental models about a product.

This exercise helps to expose people's mental models about a system. Their arrangement reveals expectations and priorities about the intended features and functions.

On separate cards, name possible features, functions or design attributes. Ask people to organize the cards logically, in ways that make sense to them.

 Example: Participants were asked to organize a vacant living room in the best possible way, to understand their priorities about luxury items in their home.

Device 114: Discover - Navigation Charts

Understand the navigation used by the participants.

This is a useful way to discover the significant elements, pathways, and other spatial behavior associated with a real or virtual environment.

Ask participants to map an existing or virtual space and understand their navigation process.

Example: The plan & schedule of courier deliveries was analyzed to understand the navigation used by them to improve efficiency.

Device 115: Discover - Cultural Differences

Ask people of different cultures to note their feelings and experiences about a specific task.

This analysis is important to understand the views, perceptions and behaviors within or across cultures.

Identify the cultures to conduct the analysis. Prepare a template diary and ask them to note their views, feelings and experiences while doing the specified activity. This information can be analyzed to understand the differences between them.

Example: To design a better dining experience the designers asked the participants to notify their views and experiences while using the dining table of their home.

Device 116: Discover - Visualize and Draw

Ask participants to visualize an experience and draw it on paper.

This exercise reveals the unspecified but important aspects of an experience. This also reveals their feelings and perception about the event.

Ask the participants to think about an experience, which would be in context of the product design and draw it on paper. The analysis of these drawing would reveal the genuine experiences and expectations of the consumers.

Example: The experiences of consumers at a bank branch were understood with the specified method to create a better environment at the branch.

About Author

Anshuman is an entrepreneur and investor and has been instrumental in nurturing many successful companies. He has created of several successful companies in various domains. He is also involved in supporting development of several other companies. In business, his interests lie in cutting edge technologies and innovative services.

His guidance has helped many businessman, investors and entrepreneurs to succeed in their businesses. He has also supported several entrepreneurship cells and incubation centers.

He is an engineer and a management graduate. He can be reached at anshuman.connect@gmail.com